You Are Accepted:

How to Get Accepted into College and Life

By Dr. Carjie Scott

You Are Accepted: How to Get Accepted into College and Life

ISBN (978-1-63848-919-1)

First Edition

Author's Note

I would like to thank all the genuine people whom I have mentioned in this book. Our relationship helped to shape who I am today. This is my story from my point of view. It reflects present memories and experiences over time. I have done my best to follow a chronological order while maintaining my truth. I am pleased to share that I have a positive relationship with everyone mentioned. I hope it remains that way.

Dedication & Acknowledgements

I dedicate this book to my mother, Carlette Walton, I hope I have made you proud. To my aunt, Evelyn Roygenia, and the rest of the village who raised me. To my cousin, Chinyere, thank you for introducing me to Mary J. Blige, Lauryn Hill, and Beyonce as their music is the soundtrack of my life. To my siblings, Ashley, Danielle, and Marc, I love you.

To my husband, Dr. Kerwin Scott, thank you for choosing me to be your wife, I couldn't do this without your unconditional love. To my children, Channing and KJ, your father and I are your *first* educators, I pray that each of you recognize the invaluable benefits of education early, listen to your teachers, and be kind to others.

To my professional colleagues and classmates, thank you for our memories.

To all of the *Carjamins* of the world, you are welcome, you are exceptional, and you are worthy and therefore, you are accepted.

I want everyone that I encounter to achieve their purpose in life, because I know that no one is here by happenstance. My life is a testament of the intimate relationship I have with God. He instructed to tell my story to *purposely* inspire others. Our lives are not just for us to live, but essentially, we are here to give of ourselves to *others*. I have chosen to give my life in this capacity.

When I had moments of despair, I questioned God, and I asked, "Why me?" God replied, "Why not, you? I have given you everything you need to defeat every enemy that comes your way. From the moment you were formed in your mother's womb, your life's purpose was established."

This book chronicles how my college education saved my life and how I conquered every adversary that attempted to derail my college career. I believe obtaining a college education may save other lives *too*.

If you've chosen to work in higher education or are considering it, this book provides insight and resourceful tools that will help you impact those you serve. The fact that you are reading these words is no coincidence. I have worked at career colleges, a top-ranked private white institution (PWI), and a historically black college and university (HBCU).

My experiences and how I responded to various situations not only tested my faith, but they awakened the sleeping giant within me. I spoke truth to power. I held leaders accountable. I was willing to fall forward. So, don't just read my story for the sake of reading it but be inspired. I hope my story gives you courage, compels you to persevere, and that it helps you to *always* do the right thing, especially when no one else is watching. Trust your instincts and work diligently to improve the education system because I want to see *all* of us thrive. Some opportunities can only be attained with a college education. Therefore, we must use our experiences to help lift others, even those who choose a path that doesn't include college attendance.

However, for those who choose or have chosen to attend college, I want you to be *completely* prepared when you are accepted to your elected college. Although I have nearly two decades of experience as a college admissions officer, I do not want you to simply enroll, but I also want you to excel, graduate, and become gainfully employed. I know each of you have the ability to transform the spaces you grace as you uplift others in your pursuit of greatness. It's imperative that we accept ourselves, because it's time to own our stories and be the change agents we need in this world!

So, join me on this literary journey, "You Are Accepted: How to Get Accepted into College and Life."

Educationally Yours,

Dr. Carjie Scott, The Education Equalizer™

Foreword

by Rosetta Miller-Perry

In the quest to improve the economic, political, and socioeconomic status of African Americans, very few factors wane in comparison when we consider the importance of higher education. It provides the requisite knowledge and training for future generations in a variety of fields. Higher education also opens doors in multiple areas and serves as a motivational force that increases one's self-esteem. It helps to obliterate stereotypes, backward generalizations, and the notions that African Americans are incapable of remarkable achievements.

Sadly, even in the 21st century, there are too many Americans who believe African Americans are unqualified to provide superior leadership and innovation. However, the increasing number of African American success stories in higher education refutes this myth. These success stories encourage and stimulate fresh outlooks and approaches to critical issues facing not only America, but the world at large.

My relationship with Dr. Carjie Scott has been one of admiration regarding her expertise and the recognition of her brilliance as a scholar and thinker. Additionally, I 've had the privilege of editing and publishing some of her critical and intriguing writings in the Tennessee Tribune. She is a constant reminder that education has immediate practical benefits and a lifelong intellectual impact. In her role as the Director of Admissions and Recruitment at Tennessee State University, she has zealously advocated the message that everyone deserves access to quality education. I am incredibly happy and proud that she launched Education Equalizers, LLC to consult students, educational leaders, and the communities they serve.

During her TSU tenure, Dr. Scott and her team in the Office of Admissions and Recruitment enrolled its highest number of first-time freshmen within the school's recent five-year history. Dr. Scott spearheaded this phenomenal milestone during a pandemic and her first year at the institution.

Dr. Scott has earned several awards, including the Karen Dolan Spirit Award and Communications Committee of the Year Award by Vanderbilt's University Staff Advisory Council. She has also been named a Nashville Emerging Leader finalist by YP Nashville and Nashville Area Chamber of Commerce.

Dr. Scott is an inspiration to African American women no matter what generation they belong to. She is a woman that conveys immense strength and integrity. Dr. Scott's drive to excel despite the obstacles she encounters is beyond commendable. Her successes have inspired me in my field as a publisher and editor. Additionally, Dr. Scott helped me understand what attributes are required to be successful in environments that blatantly scrutinize and doubt our abilities because we are African American... and even more so as a woman. This is still a severe challenge.

The Tennessee Tribune's Anthony J. Cebrun Center's journalism students have been educated by Dr. Scott to apply the following skills: in depth preparation, analytical study habits, intense concentration, and unwavering perseverance. The lessons she taught has helped in countless ways in maintaining the Tennessee Tribune as the state's premier Black-owned newspaper for more than 30 years.

Dr. Scott's experiences while managing Tennessee State University's admissions office make her the ideal person to provide insight, advice, and applicable skills to aspiring college students. She has proven through her consistently exceptional performance at TSU that she understands the mentalities and concerns of contemporary students. Consequently, Dr. Scott provides a comfortable and judgement-free zone for students to discuss their ideals regarding college, issues, goals, and what they need to have a fulfilling college experience.

Dr. Scott is a gifted writer, who is able to condense and frame complex subject matters into easily understandable and enjoyable contexts. She vividly conceptualizes the material without oversimplifying it or making it too difficult to comprehend. This makes her the perfect person to author "You Are Accepted: How to

Get Accepted into College and Life," and this text will become a definitive classic in its field.

As an African American woman, Dr. Scott has nearly two decades of professional leadership within higher education. She has navigated and continues to surmount the daily challenges of upper-level management within the world of academia. Dr. Scott's tenure at Vanderbilt University, her enlightening experiences at Tennessee State University (an HBCU), and the culmination of her expertise and educational accomplishments are presented in this book.

Her previous eBook "Attend College for Free in Tennessee," along with past articles she has written for the Tennessee Tribune and other publications pre-established her credentials and deemed her an expert in the field. This new book will expand the reach and purpose of education as we know it. Furthermore, this literary work reveals what it takes to triumph in and out of college, how to utilize academic training efficiently, and highlights the realities of life after graduation. Lastly, Dr. Scott gives realistic assessments of the economic challenges involved in higher education and how to handle them.

As someone who has met and interviewed hundreds of scholars, professors, and experts over the years, none have impressed me more than Dr. Carjie Scott. In addition to her professional repertoire, Dr. Scott is humorous, down-to-earth, and she has the ability to establish a positive rapport that allows everyone she encounters to feel at ease... regardless of their background. I cannot think of anyone who is more qualified than Dr. Scott to be the authoritative voice of, "You Are Accepted! How to get Accepted into College and Life."

Table of Contents

Prologue

"You are accepted," are the three words that college applicants yearn to hear. If you attended or considered attending college, the application process is simultaneously exhilarating and exhausting. A person's high school years is filled with defining moments that prepares them for college. Students worked diligently to pass their classes and earn exceptional grades. Many of them spent their summers visiting college campuses and took preparatory courses for the ACT or SAT.

In an effort to build their resume, students get involved in various extracurricular activities and complete several hours of community service. During their junior year, they apply to the colleges of their choice. Then, they submit their required transcripts, test scores, and perhaps a personal statement. Like most college hopefuls, they even provide letters of recommendation. Finally, their hard work has paid off!

As a senior, they celebrate as they receive *their* college acceptance letters. Everyone's preparation is different, and every applicant has their own unique story. Although, being accepted has different meanings for each of us, being accepted gives each of us the freedom to leave an indelible impression on the world; no matter what area of life we desire to be accepted into.

I have experienced my fair share of failure and heartbreak, some of it was inherited, and some was self-inflicted. Remarkably, I *still* have a 100% success rate. I overcame unbelievable odds, and I felt compelled to tell my truth as I inspire others to embrace theirs. Regardless, of how dismal, painful, or difficult your life is or has been. Please understand, that sometimes even after we've been accepted and have opportunities to sit at the table, there will be moments when we are made to feel as if we will never be welcome or have a chance to sit at the head of the table. Thus, proper preparation is imperative.

This book applauds the individuals who are the "firsts" in their family and also encourages those who desire to be "the first." Possibly, the first to move to a new city, attend college, get married, buy a home, or even the first to just believe *in yourself*!

I am telling my story for women and people of color who intend to serve in leadership positions or are currently serving, but the politics of inequity has impeded their impact. This book was not written braggadociously, but to strategically activate and identify allies who will help minorities be successful. Far too many of us have been blindsided by the inequitable and institutional practices of sexism, racism, and classism.

The defining moments I've revealed in this book, catapulted my career, and contributed to the achievement of several personal goals. Some of these instances caused me to pause and reflect; and others were shockingly unfathomable. I suffered from imposter syndrome, survivors 'guilt, cognitive dissonance, and tokenism. Historically, the higher education system in America is ladened with habitual transgressions of unfairness. If you're teachable and can relate to my lived experiences, the tools you will need to thrive as an incoming college student or higher education leader are provided here... so that we can equalize education *together*.

This narrative documents my life's experiences [personally and professionally] and explains how to get accepted into college and life as well. If you don't remember anything else from this book, remember this: "You are welcome, you are exceptional, and you are worthy. This is why you are accepted!" If you do not believe it *now*, I hope this book encourages you to believe it as you read, because everything you need to be accepted is already within you.

Chapter 1:
Own Your Story

*"You are welcome, you are exceptional, and you are worthy.
And that is why, you are accepted!"*

My college education saved my life. I grew up on the Southside of Chicago and I am the daughter of an immigrant father from Manila, Philippines, and an African American mother. My parents instilled and constantly emphasized the importance of education. Quite frequently, they presented me as their model child because I was the oldest and I maintained decent grades in school. I was the *first* person in my immediate family to earn a high school diploma and a college degree. However, I know I will not be the *last*.

My father and mother met at Dunbar High School in a GED class. In the 1980s, students who did not finish high school had to complete General Education Development courses. My parents also took the GED exam to demonstrate their knowledge of the skills that are acquired 9th-12th grade.

My upbringing was relatively modest; however, I didn't fully comprehend its' impact until my adult years. We lived in a three-flat brownstone in Bronzeville, on the southside of Chicago. Each floor had a separate apartment. My grandmother, grandfather, and mother lived on the third floor. My aunt and her daughter lived on the second floor. Our landlords lived on the first floor. Each apartment floor was identical with two bedrooms and a bathroom. We didn't have the luxury of a dishwasher, just an icebox refrigerator, a stove, a table with only two chairs, and a sink in the kitchen. The bathroom had a tub, sink, and medicine cabinet. To wash our clothes, we used a laundromat that was within walking distance. My family didn't have a car, so we depended on public transportation and usually walked to nearby grocery stores.

My mother and father were never married. My mother was a victim of domestic violence at the hands of her boyfriend that *claimed* to love her. I witnessed the violence she endured. My mother's boyfriend, who was not my father, killed her. He was a Chicago Police Officer. I saw and heard how he abused my mother, physically and verbally, often while still wearing his uniform.

A village of people raised me after my mother's murder. I was only six years old when this fatal tragedy occurred, and it changed my life *forever*. I lived on 35th and Calumet, just two houses away from Alderman Bobby Rush. He helped get my mother's story in the newspapers. It took months to find her, but with Alderman Rush's help, we did.

I was dealt an unfortunate hand at the onset of my life. Although, I could have allowed this misfortune to define me, I accepted my circumstances and made the best of them. There were countless moments in my life when I wished for the unconditional love and support that only a mother could provide. However, I am thankful that I felt a sense of purpose at a young age. So, I vowed to make my mother proud as she smiled from heaven and watched over me.

My favorite memory of my mother is of her dropping me off at pre-school. She gave the warmest hugs and kissed my forehead lovingly. As I left her presence, she would tenderly say, "Listen to your teachers and be kind to your friends." Her words of advice still resonate with me *today*, and I give my children the same instructions *daily*.

I am providing my background for purpose, not pity! There was a time when I was scared to do so. The thought of anyone knowing the horrific ugliness of my past use to paralyze me. However, as I learned to own the experiences that shaped me, the fear that I felt regarding my truth dissipated.

The college admissions process and other admittance processes requires us to own our entire story, because we must accept ourselves before anyone else will. It is easy to pretend that we have it all together all the time. Similarly, the same energy we utilize to pretend, is the same energy it takes to own our problems as we relentlessly work to solve them.

I heeded my mother's advice and I always respected my teachers. My teachers and guidance counselors encouraged and pushed me. After my mother was murdered, my aunt said that I became a "Holy Angels pet." Holy Angels was the elementary school I attended. Typically, I was the first child at school and the last to leave. I felt safe at school and flourished in club leadership and chorale. I attended private Catholic schools from kindergarten through my doctoral program. Growing up in Chicago, I was taught that private religious schools were *better* than the public schools in my neighborhood.

After high school, I attended college in Memphis, TN. I chose Christian Brothers University because it was affiliated with my high school, De La Salle Institute. When I arrived at CBU in 2003, I did not understand the commitment I had made. But I felt welcomed there. My father proudly escorted me to my dorm, in Maurelian Hall, and the next morning, I completed my admissions checklist. I registered for classes, secured financial aid, and sought work-study opportunities. My first semester went well, and I eagerly anticipated returning home to share my college experience during fall break. However, things were different at home. No one seemed to care or understand what was going on while I was away. I do not have any ill-feelings or blame them for not sharing my sentiments.

I understood that the people around me either did not go to college or had stayed in the city to attend colleges nearby. It was the first time that I felt like I probably needed to plan to find somewhere else to live after college. Although, I knew I could return home if I needed to, it was time for me to seriously plan the next few years of my life.

I have always been strategic. I understand that timing is essential to where we are supposed to be, and when we should to be there. I learned to trust my gut instincts. I wasn't sure if I would return to Chicago after graduation. It just didn't feel right. Therefore, I decided to get a job when I returned to CBU after fall break. Sometimes, leveling up requires us to move away from the community and comfort we are accustomed to having. I'm aware that this method does not work for everyone. However, if relocation is an option, don't shy away from the opportunity to experience a new place, new people, and new possibilities.

When we are the first in our family to do anything, we will inevitably experience moments that expose our inexperience. I know what imposter syndrome feels like. It seemed like every time I came home from college, I went back in time. When I arrived at my neighborhood block, it seemed as if it was simply there... waiting for me in all of its unchanged glory. Then, I'd ask myself, "Am I supposed to be here?"

5

I chose to continue my educational journey instead of returning to the path that my circumstances dictated for me. Imposter syndrome will deceive us and cause us to believe that we do not belong in spaces that are *better* than what we came from. When I feel this way, I eliminate the unwarranted feelings by reminding myself that I deserve everything I worked so diligently to obtain. I recognize that my place and position are purposeful and intentional.

When I returned to CBU, I accepted a position in the Admissions office; it went phenomenally well. I was already a campus tour guide and spent a considerable amount of time in the office assisting the admissions counselors with hosting students. The opportunity to earn money while doing what I loved seemed to be a perfect fit. This was the start of my career as a college admissions officer. I worked in the Office of Admissions for four years, while working part-time on weekends and evenings at Macy's in the ladies' shoe department.

Chapter 2:
Life *After* Graduation

"Never take anything for granted and always be prepared to show your value."

My family attended my college graduation from CBU. My aunt, who helped raise me, was probably the proudest. She beamed with joy and pride the entire weekend. As my Aunt Evelyn walked by Memphians she gloated and said, "My niece just graduated from college and I came from Chicago just to see her walk across the stage!" My father also took great pride in my accomplishment. He kept telling my brothers and sisters, "Education is very important, so please go to college." At the time, I believe my cousin, Smooch, was the only other person in my extended family who had graduated from college.

He attended an HBCU, Grambling State University. I hadn't learned much about HBCUs as a child, but as I got older and entered purposeful circles of influence, I soon realized that countless Black CEOs, doctors, lawyers, judges, and teachers had graduated from HBCUs. HBCUs are historically Black colleges and universities. They were formed when African Americans were not allowed to attend private white institutions (PWIs). The Higher Education Act of 1965 defined HBCUs as accredited colleges, started before 1964, whose primary mission is to educate Blacks.

Some people do not understand why HBCUs *still* exist because Blacks can attend any college, they want... *right*? Well according to the Atlantic (2019), the data proves; although HBCUs represent only 3% of America's four-year nonprofit colleges, HBCU alumni account for roughly 80% of Black judges and 50% of Black lawyers and doctors. Their students account for 25% of Black undergraduates who earn degrees in science, technology, engineering, and mathematics (STEM). The fact is, if HBCUs didn't exist, we'd have to create them for Black people to obtain professional careers and community. Also, while Blacks can apply to any college, they must be accepted *first*.

After graduation, an admissions counselor position became open at CBU. It was the first full-time salaried job interview I'd ever had. I didn't prepare as I should have, and I felt embarrassed after the interview. At the time, I blamed the interview committee for the outcome. I remember thinking to myself, "Why am I even required to complete an interview? I am always the first person they call to host students, prepare admit packets, and attend weekend events. I am even on the cover of the admissions brochure and academic catalog." However, I was quickly humbled when they told me that I was not offered the position. I realized that my denied access [at that particular time] was the biggest blessing of my life. I mean, if I was going to arrive at an interview and be ill-prepared, at least it was at my alma mater... I needed the grace. Additionally, that experience helped me to further understand that we should never take anything for granted and to always be prepared to show how much of invaluable asset we are.

I continued to apply for admissions jobs throughout the country but wasn't able to land an interview. I decided to research top-ranked companies to work for in Memphis. I quickly learned that it is a full-time job to apply for full-time employment. There was also added pressure because I had completed my college degree and the student loan payments were about to begin. I landed a job interview at AT&T. It was for a greeter position. I had learned from my previous interview experience to prepare for the interview thoroughly. I researched AT&T's strategic plan, and I even shared information about the U.S. Cellular and AT&T merger. I had a great interview. I did so well that the manager suggested that I consider a Retail Sales Associate position instead. The position was part-time plus commission; therefore, the pay was higher than that of a full-time greeter.

In addition to preparing for the job by researching the company, I presented myself as an asset and not a potential liability. I purchased a book titled "Getting from College to Career" by Lindsay Pollack. The original version of the book was published in 2007 and contained 90 things to do before joining the real world. The job preparedness section outlined how to land an interview, follow up after the interview, and sell yourself during the interview. I also purchased "The Resume Handbook" by Author D.

Rosenburg. It contained sample resumes for every field and cover letters to get your resume read by employers.

It felt like a dream conferred to work for a company like AT&T. They had 401K, ongoing and accessible training, a published management structure, an organizational chart, bonuses for sales, and discounts on merchandise. No one in my family had discussed the importance of contributing to a 401K; but AT&T's orientation discussed the benefits. I am glad that I heeded her advice. At every job I've ever had, I've always invested. AT&T was a great company to work for. During the first two weeks, I trained in Nashville, TN. The training headquarters was in Brentwood, TN. I loved driving to Nashville from Memphis. I fell in love with Nashville the moment I arrived. I thought to myself, "Wow, I would love to live here someday."

When I arrived at the training, I was the youngest person and the only Black female. I found this reality quite strange as a millennial. Also, no offense to the other Retail Sales Associates, but they were all nerdy. We wore AT&T blue or orange polos and khaki pants. We were given a cell phone and tablet. I was surrounded by all white men. I remember asking myself, "Did the hiring manager think I was nerdy too? Or did he try to hire someone different?" Simply put, I never told myself, "I'm, worthy of being here."

From the outside looking in, I did not fit the mold. Truthfully, I did fit in because I was just as qualified as every other white man there. I was equally excited to learn about the features of the Android versus the iPhone. We went to lunch at a restaurant in Franklin, TN... I sat at the table with 12 white men. We compared our wireless devices, reviewed the day's lessons, and discussed how to build applications. We had a great time as we engaged in 'techy' conversation. The Black female waitress who served us, looked at our group oddly. I knew what she was thinking, and she never had to utter one word. She was extremely nice and attentive to our table.

Later that evening, I went back to the restaurant and she happened to still be there. I told her what I did at AT&T and how I prepared for the interview to land the position. Looking back, I wish we had exchanged numbers. After our conversation, she told me she would apply as well. Throughout my lifetime, I have felt the need to share my story with others. I strive to intentionally lift as I climb. Kamala Harris, the first Black and south Asian American Vice President said it best when she declared, "I might be the first, but I will not be the last." I have embraced this mantra as my personal responsibility to help my community and give back by sharing my story with them.

According to the Center for American Progress (2019), Blacks face "systematically higher unemployment rates, fewer job opportunities, lower pay, poorer benefits, and greater job instability." I am providing this factual information because this must change. Blacks deserve equal opportunities to provide for their families and invest in their communities. However, as a Black woman, I know that we have to see it to believe it. We are worthy of living an abundant life even though the odds are systematically stacked against us.

Imposter syndrome *can* convince us [if we buy into it] that we have to look a certain way and be of a certain pedigree. It can make us feel like overcompensation is mandatory and as if working twice as hard is acceptable and normal. As a child, before people asked what my name was, with a quizzical look they'd shamelessly state, "What are you mixed with?" This question has stuck with me throughout my early adulthood.

Thankfully, people have evolved since the 80s. The newest generation to date, Generation Alpha, represents children born between 2010 and 2025. Studies from Business Wire (2019) indicate that Generation Alpha is the most diverse generation, and no one ethnic group will hold over 50% of the United States population by 2045. I am glad that people are becoming more diverse; perhaps this will help us judge each other by our character instead of our complexions.

Let me be clear; I do not want to sound judgmental. I understand that racism is systemic, and prejudice is learned. The NAACP, National Association for the Advancement of Colored People, defines racism as "the intersection of power and prejudice." When these those two factors are combined, we witness the generational ugliness that it has caused. However, acknowledgment is the first step to change the behavior.

I happen to have an advantage; my entire family is multiethnic. I am the only child of my mother and father, but I have siblings from both of them. I grew up with every race imaginable in my immediate family, from African American to Puerto Rican, Chinese, to Filipino, Mexican, Jewish, and Polish. I have always considered a person's integrity beyond the color of their skin. Unfortunately, I took this for granted when I assumed that most people valued a person's character before dismissing them because of their race. I have learned the hard way that this is not the case.

AT&T was a great experience of professional growth and development; however, I still desired to work in college admissions. I realized how important attending college was in my life, and I wanted to help others attain their college experience. Nelson Mandela said, "Education is the most powerful weapon you can use to change the world." My college experience was impactful because it taught me that learning is not limited to the classroom. It placed me in circles of influence, and it helped me dream *bigger*. My role models changed, and my values changed even more.

My degree made me feel respected and provided me with a marketable tool to help me land prospective jobs. I knew my education was an asset to help me escape poverty. "There are three ways to keep people impoverished: take away their self-esteem, take away their resources, and take away their role models," Kanye West. If I hadn't attended college, I am not sure where I would be. Therefore, I've vowed to help more students *like me* get accepted into college.

Chapter 3:
Who Are You?

"It's not about who you know but who knows you."

I applied for numerous jobs and then I finally landed a position at a school called TechSkills. TechSkills was a for-profit trade school with locations nationwide. While I didn't understand the difference between for-profit and non-profit colleges, I understood that educational institutions like TechSkills served students who wanted to earn certifications and work in the information technology industry. This industry was booming. During my tenure at TechSkills, I worked as an admissions counselor. I made lifelong friends there. Like AT&T, I had comprehensive training, a structured organizational chart, and clear opportunities for advancement.

At AT&T, I was given scripts and training manuals to sell products to customers. This helped me excel at TechSkills, and I was valued for the technology and sales language I acquired while working at AT&T. I understood customer needs and showed them how TechSkills could help them reach those needs. My students were predominantly working adults who enrolled to have promotional opportunities within their Information Technology careers.

My enthusiasm within the position dwindled quickly because I was bored with it. I talked with my boss about my long-term goals, and he encouraged me to apply elsewhere. He promised that we would work together again, and he encouraged me pursue career advancement. At the time, I didn't know my boss was also seeking employment somewhere else.

My mother's daily instructions to listen to my teachers and be nice to my friends is a practice I've applied in my life and the workplace. Nearly every job I've had is because of the relationships I built. My TechSkills boss was a great man and became my first higher education mentor. He took me under his wing and taught me everything he knew about college admissions. He also introduced me to other women in the field. Women that are now a part of my family. These women invested in me personally and professionally and have cheered me on throughout my career. My mentor and I had such a great relationship, and I knew he would be proud of me when I told him that I was ready to move on. Our relationship was a blessing and because of his leadership, I invested in my team when I became a leader, just like he had invested in me.

I landed a job at ITT Technical Institute in 2008. When I told my family that I got that job, they were proud of me, partly because it was a college with a recognizable name. I remember watching ITT Tech commercials: *Building an Education for the Future.* My mother and grandmother didn't attend traditional four-year colleges; they attended trade schools. I felt that I was doing a great service to others by working at ITT Tech. After all, we were "building an education for the future." Like AT&T and TechSkills, ITT Tech conducted a new employee orientation and had 401K plans, insurance, and tuition discount programs.

I remember going to ITT Tech for the first time. When I parked on the campus, I arrived at a box-shaped building with the ITT Tech logo on the front door. There was a receptionist with a black name board. On the board was a list of all of the students who were visiting ITT Tech that day. On the wall behind her were the accreditation and governing board certificates. On her desk was a phone and a computer. The lobby was chicly designed, and the tables had magazines related to technology, science, and business.

After the interview, I was given a tour of the building. I saw the classrooms and equipment. Then I met some of the employees and potential students. The admissions representatives were sharply dressed. Interested students had admissions overviews in the interview rooms. The interview rooms had one computer, a desk, and two chairs. The setup made TechSkills seem laughable. At ITT Tech, everything was pristine in comparison. The admissions personnel interviewed students for enrollment and

17

then escorted them to financial aid to discuss affordable tuition options.

I was offered the Admissions representative job at ITT Tech. I sat in a cubicle with other representatives. Like TechSkills, we received lists of potential students to call and share information. We had appointment goals to maintain daily. Students enrolled annually during four specified dates. When I advised students on the phone, I felt like their counselor. I understood what they wanted for their lives, and I made sure that I thoroughly articulated what ITT had to offer. I took great pride in my role, and I enjoyed working at ITT Tech, but I wanted more. It was a redundant job.

Although I helped several students, I needed to establish a long-term plan that was more gratifying. I planned to work at ITT Tech, get my Master's degree with the tuition discount, and become a Director of Recruitment. One of my ITT Tech mentors had attended Webster University. I had planned to follow her career path and enroll there as well.

About six months into the role, I began to hear about students that had sued ITT Tech for fraud and unethical financial aid practices. I began to research this, and it was true. When I learned of this, I had already been promoted to a Senior II Admissions Representative position. At ITT Tech, employees were promoted based upon the number of students we enrolled. I started as an Admissions Representative earning $36,000 and became a Senior II Admissions Representative earning $47,500 in under six months. I needed the money. I had just signed a lease for an apartment and purchased a new car. I couldn't just quit when I became privy to ITT's unethical practices. I attempted to justify my position there by focusing on the students that obtained jobs after graduation, despite my knowledge of the students who had been taken advantage of.

My dilemma epitomized Leon Festinger's (1957) cognitive dissonance theory. Cognitive dissonance is a theory used to identify the mental anguish that occurs after experiencing two conflicting attitudes or beliefs. I could no longer continue to work for an organization that did not align with my values and goals. I changed my plan. Instead of remaining at ITT Tech and becoming a Director of Recruitment, I decided to apply for other jobs and leave for-profit education.

In 2016, approximately seven years after I had resigned, ITT Tech filed for bankruptcy. Former colleagues told me that all 130 campuses nationwide closed down abruptly. The employees and students were not given any notice. It was a terrible situation for everyone involved. I was shocked to hear of the lack of planning and concern for all of the people who had invested in the company and all of the students that had studied or been currently studying there.

In 2020, The New York Times reported, ITT Tech students in Delaware would get $330 million in student loan relief. Currently, more lawsuits continue to be filed to help relieve student loan debt. This was a horrific reality for the students and the employees who worked for ITT Tech. The Indianapolis Business Journal (2016) reported that over 8,000 employees lost their jobs. Two employees filed a federal action lawsuit. They claimed that the company violated federal law by not providing a 60 days' notice. No settlement for employees has been made yet.

Thankfully, I was not affected by the closure. I was able to leave ITT Tech in 2009. My former boss and mentor from TechSkills called me with a job offer at Cambridge College. The main campus was located in Boston, MA; and I was going to work for the satellite campus in Memphis, TN. I was glad that I had recently received a promotion at ITT Tech. It helped me to negotiate my salary at Cambridge for the Admissions Counselor position. Cambridge College was a traditional non-profit graduate school. Its primary mission was to educate teachers and administrators. The programs consisted of Master of Education, Certificate of Graduate Study, and Doctor of Education.

I connected with great students at Cambridge, and I felt like I was truly giving back by helping them. I felt fulfilled in this role. I traveled across West TN to share information with future educators. I worked weekdays and weekends. There was a 401K plan, insurance, and tuition reimbursement but no training manual. The only training I received was from my boss. After networking with others at Cambridge, I learned that it is common to receive on the job training from peers instead of an official trainer at traditional colleges. It was also common for administrators to earn less money than faculty. I didn't need the training because I could apply what I had learned from previous roles. However, I desired to make more money.

Dear reader, I want to remind you that I had moved from Chicago to Memphis for college. I had also worked in the admissions office and retail sales throughout my four years of undergrad. After I graduated, I decided to live in Memphis. I consider myself one of the lucky ones. According to NPR.org (2019), "just 58 percent of students who started college in the fall of 2012 had earned a degree six years later." I was able to graduate, land four jobs, and continue to increase my salary. My salary enabled me to live in my own apartment, purchase a new car, pay bills, and afford my weekend activities. After college graduation, employment is not guaranteed. As a result, I felt a heightened sense of pressure to prove my college experience was worth my time. After all, I was the first in my family to attend college. About six out of 10 students who start college [...] will be saddled with student debt without the earning potential to pay it off" (NPR.org, 2019). Thankfully, I was not included in this statistic. I am afraid of what could have happened if I were. However, this is when survivors' guilt started to develop.

Survivor's guilt made me feel like I didn't deserve the life I lived. I had peers who had attended CBU with me, some of them graduated, while others didn't. It seemed that many of them were still trying to find themselves and their purpose. It had been three years since we had graduated. When I shared my accomplishments with them, they were happy for me. However, I felt bad when I shared my accomplishments. My college friends did not have the same struggles as I did. When we were in college together, they had more support and families that expected them to come home for the holidays. They knew my life story and they witnessed my transformation. Although we were great friends, ironically, I felt guilty for surviving and thriving. I felt as though my happiness and success were interpreted as bragging. It was easy to share my obstacles, but it was hard to share what I had overcome.

At my core, I have always been a teacher. When I see gaps, I try to close them. If I know more than someone else, I will teach them what I know. My attitude has carried me my entire life and it is celebrated and welcomed by people who want to learn. The great thing about Cambridge College was I could be innovative and creative in the role. I created a training manual for our office. Our location was technically a startup, so we were able to set the foundation. I felt empowered to set the tone and make things happen. It was probably one of the best jobs I had at the beginning of my career.

I had planned to get my master's from Cambridge, but I learned that I had a balance at CBU. I couldn't retrieve my transcripts until I satisfied my debt. So, I saved money until I had enough to rectify the balance. Although I loved working at Cambridge, I became anxious about it. At the time, it was the longest job I had. However, my personal life was in shambles. My friends truly admired me, and it felt like I became the mother hen of our circle. I couldn't handle the pressure. They would ask for advice about relationships and jobs. Our roles shifted. I used to ask them for that advice. I didn't think that I was the *right* person to offer guidance to anyone [in that capacity].

Chapter 4:
You Don't Belong Here

"Nearly everything I tried had failed."

I joined a church and focused on what I desired personally, this included the type of relationships I wanted, where I wanted to live, and the kind of friend I wanted to be. I believe the issues of my past began to surface. I could no longer mask my personal traumas with success. I wanted to start fresh. I didn't know where I would go; I just knew that I wanted to be content in all areas of my life. So, I packed up my apartment and put all of my belongings at my front door. Later that day, a friend came over and asked, "Carj, where are you going?" I responded, "I don't know. I just want to get out of here." A few weeks went by, and my old boss from ITT Tech called. He had a position for Director of Admissions at Anthem Career College in Atlanta, GA. The pay was twice the salary I made, and the company was willing to pay all of the expenses associated with my relocation. I was intrigued by the opportunity and the chance to meet new people.

I never imagined that I could make that much money, and I didn't know that companies willingly paid for relocation. My immaturity made me value the opportunity to move and make more money over anything else. Since my former boss already knew my capacity, there was not a real interview process, and I was already packed to leave. However, the scandals at ITT Tech caused me to question if I was making the right decision. The year was 2009, and ITT Tech was still open. I also remembered my plan to stay in a non-profit. Consequently, I told my former boss at Cambridge that I was being considered for another opportunity. He reluctantly gave me his blessing and said his infamous words for the second time, "we will work together again." Then I moved to Atlanta, GA.

It was a huge mistake. I should've followed my plan and faced my personal issues head-on. Unbeknownst to me, Anthem Career College was formerly High-Tech Institute. High-Tech Institute had changed its name to Anthem Career College because they experienced the same lawsuits that ITT Tech had. I was a fish out of water. This was the hardest job I ever had. I had gone from being the best in admissions to the worst. It seemed as though I didn't know how to handle anything. Nearly everything I tried had failed.

We were located near the Lindbergh exit of the Marta transit line, in a newly developed shopping area. Our campus was right above Wet Willie's. The only good thing that happened while I was employed at Anthem was meeting my mentor. This woman was a badass! She called me out on my issues, and we had countless therapy sessions. She challenged me to embody my greatness and she believed in me. My mentor had relocated from the Anthem College in Nashville, TN. One night, we went to my boss's house by invitation to discuss the day's work. We had all relocated from TN and lived near each other.

My boss was drunk and was dressed inappropriately. He was wearing flimsy thigh-high shorts and a t-shirt. It appeared that he didn't have any underwear on, and his breath smelled like liquor. She called him out on it in a very respectful way. I was shocked when he came to the door. I had never experienced anything like that and froze when I laid eyes on him. We were probably there for five minutes before we left, and I was so glad that my mentor and I were together that night. She set him straight and we used that moment to establish boundaries with him in our professional relationship.

At Anthem, I had a team of admissions counselors and front desk staff. It was my first Director of Admissions role. I had to hire them, train them, and hold them accountable for their outcomes. One of my employees had a drug problem. That employee came to me and asked for their paycheck to be cut early. I remember that person coming into my office and scratching their neck. I went to my boss and mentioned the interaction. My boss cut his final check. That was the first person I ever fired.

We were not meeting our enrollment numbers; so, the corporate offices required that we check in weekly with our performance metrics. My daily duties required me to report the total number of students in our enrollment funnel, the number of students who visited campus, the number of students who committed to attending, and the number of students who actually attended. Weekly, I participated in a call to discuss those outcomes. I was able to gain a better understanding of how for-profit colleges worked and how they valued numbers more than people.

We had several issues. One, we received the same leads from former High-Tech Institute students. Two, I let the pressures of the numbers and reporting harm my relationships with my teammates. Three, my boss started to resent his decision of hiring me and blamed me for everything that went wrong.

This leadership position helped me to understand the true nature of the college admissions business. I was privy to public and private conversations. Some of those conversations brought out the best in people, and others brought out the worst. I had a seat at the table. I did all the hiring and firing. I chose salaries. I had full control of the lives of people. I never had that much power. I wanted to use it for good, but I was not experienced enough to efficiently maximize my authority. I learned that potential students have the power, not the admissions offices. There is no school without students, and applicants are only competing with each other. This lesson is consistent with all higher education entities.

My admissions team complained that the callers hung up on them or they complained about the issues that High-Tech Institute never reconciled. Due to my high-stress level that was caused by trying to increase our numbers, my move to Atlanta, and my unresolved personal issues, I made the necessary phone calls and did all the work myself. I lashed out at my team and didn't work with them or help them. I was so focused on my success that I was dismissive of theirs. Since my boss blamed me, I blamed my team.

My Anthem mentor told me, "Car, you are doing the best you can. Don't be so hard on yourself. Don't give up." But giving up was all that was left because I had never failed so badly before. I had never had a job that I didn't excel in. And I had never let anyone down as badly as I had let all of these people down. So, I quit that job and moved back to Memphis. This was the greatest failure of my life. I should have researched that job before I accepted it. I fell flat on my face. It was 2011, and I was in that role for only seven months.

In 2014, Anthem Career College was unable to resell to investors and abruptly closed down. Students and employees filed class-action lawsuits. Kamaria Hubert, an Anthem Career College student in Memphis, was interviewed by WMC Channel 5 News, "I have five kids. That's the reason I went on and decided to go to school so that I could get a higher-paying career and provide better care for my children."

When I left Anthem in 2011, I felt miserably defeated. However, my relationship with God was starting to develop. I had known of God; but admittedly, I was a part-time Christian. I seemed to only focus on the Bible verses about prosperity. I didn't read the scriptures from start to finish, so I didn't apply the wisdom found within God's word properly. I memorized the lines that applied to me. For example, Jeremiah 29:11 (KJV) states, "For I know the plans I have for you says the Lord, plans to prosper you and to give you a hope and a future." However, upon a thorough analysis of that scripture, I realized that God does not promise to rescue us from a situation immediately; instead, God reminds us that He has a purpose and promise for our lives. I believe that I picked up the Bible because I was in mourning because of the calamities within my career. I needed a guide to navigate me during that low point in my life. At that time, neither school had closed down; but I knew it was inevitable.

This was the first time that I turned to God and asked for forgiveness. Before my failure, I treated God like He was Santa Claus. I have learned that God is much more than a powerful being that answers prayer requests. It wasn't until I started reading the Bible in its entirety that I understood. In Jeremiah 29:11, I learned that God said those words to a group of people while they suffered in Babylon. For context, their suffering lasted 70 years! I learned that God wanted me to be whole, and if that required me to remain in a place that I wanted to leave... God would not rescue me *immediately.*

I was so traumatized by my failure at Anthem that it took me several months to find a new job in Memphis. In instances like these, it doesn't matter how much we've prepared; it is hard to sell ourselves in an interview when we have been beaten down. The partner of a former student that I had recruited to attend Cambridge, learned that I had moved back to Memphis and was hiring. I landed a job with her at Chrichton College, a small-private Christian College in Memphis, TN. I was an Outreach Coordinator. It was less than half of the salary I earned at Anthem. However, I redeemed myself and quickly found my stride. I was grateful for the job and needed to be lifted again. I was elated to be working for a non-profit private Christian college. We were even required to attend church, but I didn't mind because I had a ton of things to pray about.

A few months after I got this role, Chrichton College was purchased by a for-profit company and was renamed Victory University. The new owners claimed that the college would remain religious but would be for-profit. The wind was knocked out of me. I had spent a ton of money breaking my lease in Atlanta, moving my furniture back to Memphis, and time to restore myself from my experience working in for-profit. Although, I tried to be optimistic, things went down-hill quickly. I realized that non-profit private schools would have to align their accounting practices and use business models of for-profit institutions if they wanted to remain open. The leaders at Chrichton College hoped for the best but received the worst. Ultimately, Victory University formerly Chrichton College closed in 2014.

I felt so bad for my boss at Chrichton College. Her name was Mrs. (Dr.) TaMara Madden. She was an alumnus of Chrichton College. She was just a few years older than me and was full of life and passion. Her smile lit up the room. She was a huge supporter of my success and the success of everyone around her. While on a walk in our Cordova neighborhood, she passed away due to natural causes. I know that she is smiling down on me from heaven. She was a wife and mother, and her life ended much too soon.

Like ITT Tech and Anthem, I was able to leave Victory University before they closed. I landed a job at Vatterott Career College as the Director of Admissions. I rebounded. Vatterott Career College was a for-profit institution based out of St. Louis. I researched Vatterott and was impressed that the school offered programs that my grandmother and mother studied when they attended trade school. My grandmother was a medical assistant, and my mother was a cosmetologist. Vatterott offered programs in healthcare, business, cosmetology, and nursing. My former mentor from ITT Tech was the Regional Director of Admissions.

I killed it at Vatterott. I exceeded every goal, and I had the lowest admissions turnover in the company. I earned two awards and my salary increased every year. I rewarded my team. I held them accountable, and I gave much more grace than I did while I was at Anthem Career College. I served at Vatterott for four years. My boss and I talked about my career opportunities and she believed in me too! We went to church together and our relationship evolved organically. We became extremely close. I viewed my boss as a parental figure. She was one of the most understanding and patient bosses I ever had. I learned so much from her. She was loved by all the employees because she knew how to lead without being bossy! She motivated us, cultivated relationships, and invested in our success. During my third year at Vatterott, a Regional Director of Admissions position became available. The job required that I train other Directors of Admissions and serve as the Campus President when necessary. I would work directly for the corporate offices and report to the Vice President and CEO in this role. It was no secret that I had planned to apply for it. In fact, my boss encouraged me to do so.

I felt like my life was on a better path; it was 2014, and I had accumulated about a decade of admissions experience. Even my personal life was thriving. One weekend during the summer, my best friend invited me to a bar-be-que. She had just pledged to a sorority. It was a fraternity party; so, I was hesitant to attend. I remember thinking, I am not in a Greek letter organization; I will probably be forced to sit alone while everyone else strolled the scene happily and danced to the latest R&B hits. However, when my phone buzzed displaying the address to the bar-be-que, I decided to go.

I had purchased a new dress off Beale street and had recently bought a blue Toyota FJ Cruiser. It was a beautifully warm day, and I drove with the windows down. I met my friend at the party. When I arrived, the scene was exactly as I expected; everyone sat with their Greek affiliates and I sat quietly on the corner of a couch and watched the BET awards. I happened to glance across the room. I saw some guys playing cards. One of the guys looked at me; he even pulled his glasses down and gave a long stare. He was handsome, and I waved. He didn't wave back, I turned around, and there was a wall behind me. I was confused because I knew he didn't just glance at me, his eyes lingered. I shrugged it off and continued watching the BET Awards.

When the crowd of people began to do their strolls and calls, I left. My girlfriend walked me to my car. The guy from the table followed us. He stopped my friend and asked her if he could walk me to my car. As destiny orchestrated, I've been with him ever since. After a year of dating, I announced my pregnancy and upcoming wedding on Halloween to my Vatterott boss. At the time, there were three other pregnant employees on our campus. My boss simply smiled and said, "there must be something in the

33

water." My husband was so excited that we were having a baby. He was very considerate and attended every hospital visit with me. He brought lunch to my job and sometimes he dropped me off at work in the mornings. He became a member of the Vatterott family. Everybody knew him.

We got married in 2013, during Martin Luther King Jr. weekend. Our closest friends and family attended. My father walked me down the aisle. His mom and dad said a special prayer. We were married by our Life Church pastor. It was a packed event, and we danced the night away. We decided to purchase a home in East Memphis. We lived on Woodcrest Drive near the Botanical Gardens. We were both first-time homeowners. My pregnancy went well, and we had a healthy baby girl. When I held her in my arms, my entire world changed. Life as I knew it ended, and my family life began.

I was the first in my family to own a home. Since the inception of this country, Blacks have been excluded from quality education, housing, and healthcare. "We have created a caste system in this country, and African Americans are exploited and geographically separated by racially explicit government policies. Although most of these policies are now off the books, they have never been remedied, and their effects endure," Richard Rothstein *The Color of Law*.

As Black people, we are still trying to climb out of the hole we were buried in... and we are treated as if our desire to provide for our families and create generational wealth is problematic. Arne Duncan, former Secretary of Education and native Chicagoan said, "Race, social and economic status, zip code, or the neighborhood shouldn't matter. Every child desperately needs and deserves a chance to get a great education." Therefore, a child in America will only have a chance at a quality education if they are born in an affluent zip code, or their parents can afford to send them to a private school.

My family was able to pay for my private education through high school, but they could not pay for my college education. I did not want the same fate for my daughter. I wanted her to attend great schools, witness a healthy marriage, and start life with a decent deck of cards. While on maternity leave, I saw Vatterott on the news. A student had complained that classes were in session, but no teacher was present. I enjoyed time with my new family, but I was ready to return to work and receive my promotion. One evening, my boss texted and said that I did not get the Regional Admissions Director role because of my pregnancy.

I learned that Vatterott hired someone else to be Regional Director of Admissions in my office while I was on leave. I was devasted. All the long hours, all the admissions success awards, all the accolades and praise were worthless at that moment. I was a new mother, wife, and homeowner on maternity leave. I remember thinking, "Wow, they replaced me in a heartbeat. This company does not care about me at all." It was a hard pill to swallow.

I thought I had such a great relationship with my boss. I could not believe that she did not convince the hiring manager to give me the position. Maybe she did, and they didn't care. I don't know. I was afraid to say anything, but I knew that I had to do something because it just wasn't fair. I knew if I reported what my boss told me, then I would risk our friendship. It was scary because I needed my job, and I thought they might fire me since I had held them accountable. I hated being caught in the middle of this situation, but I had to stand up for myself and my new family.

I finally got the courage to file a claim with the Equal Employment Opportunity Commission. I began to think about all of the employees from colleges like ITT Tech and Anthem. I thought about how they actually cared about the students but lost their jobs because of poor corporate leadership. I was upset because I had given the company almost four years of my life, and they dismissed me because I was finally doing something for myself. If I had the Regional Director role, I could teach admissions teams to recruit the *right way*. I might even have enough influence to keep teachers in the classroom. Also, I'd have the capability to help students like my grandmother and mother. After all, if these schools didn't exist, then where would the students attend?

I took my baby with me to the EEOC Office. It was the hardest and scariest thing I had ever done. However, I embodied the strength that I witnessed from my Anthem Career College mentor when she stood up to our boss. I went to the office, and I filed a claim. I had to tell the EEOC representative the full story. I gave the representative every detail. I had shown all of my performance reviews. I almost changed my mind in that office because I had to list the name of my boss. For a moment, I was more concerned about my boss than myself. I did not want my boss to get into trouble. But I had a family to take care of, and I had to let Vatterott know that this was not fair. The EEOC sent a letter to Vatterott. And upon my return from maternity leave, I was offered the position. I was making more than I had ever made, and I was proud that I had stood up for myself. Sadly, my relationship with my boss deteriorated, and it was painful. I served in the Regional Director of Admissions position for a year and was promoted again to Director of Education overseeing 50 employees at the second largest campus in Vatterott Nation.

Chapter 5:
How Bad Do You Want It?

"People thought that we were out of our minds"

When my husband and I met, we talked beside my car after the bar-be-que, he told me that he wanted to be a Dentist. I replied, "Wow, a DDS, you look like a Dentist. He smiled the biggest smile and was impressed that I knew what a DDS was." He is still so easy to please. He says I'm the smartest woman he has ever met; he loves to flatter me. When I met him, he worked for the Social Security Administration.

He had been trying to get into dental school for several years. When he graduated from high school, he spent four years in the Marine Corps, attended a community college and transferred to Lane College. Lane College is an HBCU in Jackson, TN. He graduated from Lane Magna Cum Laude with a Biology degree. He continued to apply for professional and dental programs while working for SSA and his mentor. His mentor is an Oral Surgeon with his own private office. My husband never gave up on his dream and was eventually admitted to Meharry Medical College for a Master's degree in Health Administration.

It was tough to move to Nashville with a small child, a new mortgage in Memphis, and no job. But we did it. I left Vatterott, we packed our house, and we moved into a small apartment near

North Nashville. People thought that we were out of our minds. No one knew that we were moving so that my husband could pursue his dream.

I think that most people assumed that he had been admitted to Dental school. Although the program prepared students to become dentists, there was a slight chance that he wouldn't get accepted into the dental program. In 2015, a week before we left to move to Nashville, I landed a job interview at Vanderbilt University for an associate director position. The first interview was conducted via a teleconference with HR, the second interview was completed virtually with the hiring manager, and I relocated to Nashville before the final interview was confirmed.

My husband, 2-year-old daughter, and I arrived in Nashville, TN. We moved into a small apartment near Meharry Medical College. One night, while my husband studied, I broke down in tears. He was at school and I had not secured a job yet, so we lived off our savings. However, I needed some help.

I booked an appointment at Vanderbilt University to tour the campus. I had never visited Vanderbilt before but heard great things about it. I remember walking on campus with the group. A current student led our tour. She was dressed in black and gold and was so proud of the University. She gave a thorough overview of the programs, the buildings, and athletics. It was a beautiful campus. I had never seen anything like it. I prayed for God to give me the job that I had interviewed for a few weeks ago.

We found a daycare for my daughter the next day. I continued to apply for positions. Then Vanderbilt called me for my final interview. It was three hours long, and I met with over six people. It was tough, but I prepared well. They offered me the job immediately after my final interview. I was ecstatic. In my eyes, Vanderbilt was perfect. It was everything I could have imagined. I was so proud of myself. Working at Vanderbilt made me feel like all of my hard work had paid off.

I went from working at Vatterott Career College to Vanderbilt University. For context, I was literally working at a college in a strip mall and ended up working at one of the top colleges in the country. I thought I had finally made it. All of the years I worked in for-profit and small non-profit colleges had meaning. I knew there was no way that I'd have to endure the things I experienced at other colleges.

I remember how I felt walking on that campus. It was one of the proudest moments of my life. Like AT&T, I felt like an outsider, but I found people that I had common interests with and made friends quickly. I remember going home to tell my family and friends that I was an associate director at Vanderbilt. My father was so proud of me. He said, "You made it Pump. That's a great job.

You should retire from there." He encouraged me to go back to school. He said, "You should be a doctor or my personal attorney." Any chance I had to bring my family to the campus, I did; I was just in awe at the buildings and the intellectuals that I had access to. I enrolled in the meal plan; I became involved with free events on campus, and I wore Vanderbilt colors. I felt so honored that they had chosen me. To state I was happy is an understatement.

I accumulated a decade of experience before working for Vanderbilt. I had managed teams of five to 50 people. I had led the admissions and academic affairs departments. I had roles that required me to report directly to the CEO. I worked at a startup campus. I was a hiring manager. I had broken admissions records. I was well-known in Memphis as a trusted higher education professional. I was seasoned with my fair share of wins and lessons. With my experience, I knew I would be a valued asset at Vanderbilt.

I began at Vanderbilt in 2015. At the time, Vanderbilt had just started an Equity, Diversity, and Inclusion (EDI) office. I was impressed with the office. I thought that it was forward-thinking of Vanderbilt to have a dedicated team of people committed to EDI. I assumed that an office like that meant that Vanderbilt was "sincerely" committed to a diverse workspace. While I worked at Vanderbilt, the EDI office had three different leaders. Every year the former leader was replaced. I was naïve and believed that maybe they were choosing the wrong person for the job. It made me want to learn more about the office. I figured maybe I could serve there too.

One of my favorite perks was being able to work set hours and be home by 5 pm. I needed a set schedule because I had to pick up my daughter from school. I also had to adjust to my husband being away from home most of the time. However, my husband noticed that I was having a difficult time with the move and our baby. I was used to being with him and having family and friends to depend on. He found a babysitter and started to bring me around his classmates. I quickly learned the benefits of an HBCU education. It was the first time that I had ever been around so many successful Black people.

I loved his classmates. Just thinking about them brings so much joy to my heart. They made me feel like I was enrolled at Meharry. They were very respectful of our relationship and kept me in the loop about everything that happened. I don't believe my husband could have chosen a better group of people to study with. It truly felt like a family. I am still best friends with many of his classmates.

Vanderbilt University is just a few blocks away from Meharry Medical College. When we moved to Nashville from Memphis, it was a culture shock. Both cities are in Tennessee.

However, Memphis is predominately Black, and Nashville is white. The contrast between the two cities is glaring. Memphis is a great city; however, the available resources are scarce in comparison to Nashville. My co-workers from Vanderbilt seemed to be fascinated with my husband. He is a 6'4 tall, dark, and handsome Black man. Every time he visited me at work for lunch, they were enamored with him. It "seemed" that my department welcomed my entire family.

In previous roles, I had my own office, with a window and privacy. At Vanderbilt, I shared a workspace in an area that was formerly a closet. The room had no windows, and my suitemate preferred that we use lamps instead of the light. I obliged. Also, the office was already decorated with *her* things. It looked like a Kirkland's storefront, but I didn't complain. I understood that she had the space before me, and the decorations were suitable.

Like Cambridge and Chrichton, my training was on the job. I noticed a trend. This was the third non-profit school that I had to create my own training manual. I learned from everyone around me. Unlike any other job I had, everyone that I assisted had different expectations. As time went on, it seemed like everyone was my boss. I did not have a team to report to me. I was in a catch-all position. I supported operations for multiple programs, including budgets, report building, logistics, marketing, and communications. I was also a manager for a consortium of top-ranked business schools. I had many different tasks for several different programs, and it was quite difficult for me to master anything. My workload was tremendous!

Chapter 6:
How College Admissions "and Life" Works

*"Always check the class profile **and** the census of people around you"*

My primary responsibility at Vanderbilt was to track and input data, specifically the students that had expressed interest in the university. I learned how traditional admissions offices actually worked. They are quite similar to for-profit offices. It is a numbers game. Let's say that 100 students apply to a college. Out of the 100, 50 of the applications are incomplete. An incomplete application does not have the required documents such as: transcripts, essays, or test scores. Admissions coordinators contact students with incomplete applications to assist them with the submission of these documents. The other 50 are complete. Of the complete applications, some applicants are local, some are international, some meet the admissions requirements, and some exceed the admissions requirements. Some are men, some are women, some are athletes, some are military, some are student body presidents, some are valedictorians, and some have identified their race. Some students receive a scholarship, and some have to apply for loans. The completed applications receive a decision. The students who receive an admit decision create the class profile.

The class profile helps determine how many students an admissions office will admit and the overall scholarship budget. Admissions officers vet the completed applications to determine which students meet the class profile. The class profile is used to assess the overall application pool. When students meet the minimum average characteristics, they are contacted by admissions officers for admittance or a follow up interview. When applying for college, always ask for the class profile and average amount of scholarship award issued. This will inform you of the types of students that are generally admitted into the institution and determine the cost associated with college attendance. I have provided you with a sample generic class profile worksheet (Table 1). The worksheet is not the same for all institutions.

Table 1. Sample Generic Class Profile Worksheet

In-State	75%	These students live in the state that the university is located. They pay the least in tuition because of government grants and in-state funding.
Out-of-State	15%	These students live out of state. These students will pay out of state fees, which brings more money to the university. Select schools offer discounted tuition for students who live within a designated radius from the university.
International	10%	These students do not live in the United States. They have other admissions requirements that require transcript translation and must apply for student visas to study in the US. These students are usually self-pay, which brings more money to the university. International students also help to create global name recognition for the university.
Average GPA	3.3	When applying for college, always research the average GPA to determine if you meet the minimum admissions standards. If the average GPA is 3.3, it is likely that you will need at least a 3.3 to be considered and greater that a 3.3 to be competitive.

Table 1. continued.

Average ACT Score	25	When applying for college, always research the average test scores to determine if you meet the minimum admissions standards. If the average ACT is 25, it is likely that you will need at least a 25 to be considered and greater that a 25 to be competitive. You do not need to submit an ACT and SAT. You can submit either test. You should submit the test with the higher score.
Average SAT Score	1075	If the average SAT is 1075, it is likely that you will need at least a 1075 to be considered and greater that a 1075 to be competitive. Most East Coast students take the SAT.
Male	65%	Admissions offices consider gender when admitting. What is important to you? Do you want to attend a college with more men or women?
Female	35%	Admissions offices consider gender when admitting. Sometimes there are scholarships available based on gender.
White (non-Hispanic)	80%	Admissions offices consider race when admitting. What is important to you? Do you want to attend a college with a diverse student body?
Black or African American, Native American, Asian, and Pacific Islander (Minorities)	20%	Depending upon the college, Black, Native American, Asian, etc. students might be the minority. Do you want to attend a college where you are the minority? Have you researched the programs offered to support students you identify with?

Admissions offices consider these variables during the admissions process to some degree. This is how admissions offices create their student body. PWIs maintain their class profile to strategically create their incoming student cohorts. They can forecast their application pool and determine their class profile based upon received applications. In for-profit institutions, it's similar; however, the difference is the admissions standards.

For-profit institutions usually have open admissions standards. They are not necessarily interested in creating a class profile; instead, they want to admit as many students as possible. Therefore, when for-profit admissions offices review candidates, they review the total number of inquiries, the type of contacts made with those inquiries, and the response rate when contacting potential students. They forecast their enrollment class before students have applied. Whereas most traditional universities forecast their enrollment numbers after students have been admitted and have confirmed their intent to enroll. Many public universities, HBCUs, and community colleges have open admissions standards as well. Generally, if you meet their posted requirements, you will get admitted.

During my first year, I didn't meet my boss's expectations. She was a tough leader. She told me, "You just don't have an operations skillset, you should take classes to improve your writing ability, and you don't pay attention to detail." I listened to her. Admittedly, I spent a lot of time asking questions. I was curious about the lack of minority students enrolled in our department. I needed to understand why those numbers were stagnant. When I questioned this, I typically received responses like, "Minority students have low test scores, or they just aren't interested in our school." She had data to support her claims.

I respected her and I valued her honesty regarding my performance. Admittedly, I never had a boss like her. She was definitely the smartest boss I ever had. I appreciated her constructive criticism. In fact, I thrived off of it. It challenged me to push harder. I stopped asking questions that weren't related to my job. Instead, I focused on the work that was assigned to me. I was determined to improve; so, I enrolled in communications and excel courses.

My progress wasn't a quick process. We continued having one-on-one sessions, and oftentimes I wanted to give up. However, I saved every "kudos" email I got. I documented all of the processes I created, and I provided solutions. She started to appreciate my strategic mindset and gave me more projects. The most impactful project was leading a group of underprivileged youth. They visited the campus every summer to learn about business school. Each year my presentation got better and better. At the last presentation, I invited my husband to join. He spoke with me while dressed in his white coat. The kids loved it; I still have relationships with some of them. I witnessed how hard it was to recruit top students of color. Most of them choose higher-ranking schools. Unfortunately, I was not in a recruitment role, so I couldn't help full-time. My primary job was in operations and the needs of the back office were my priority. However, when asked, I offered advice on how to properly recruit within diverse spaces.

Every day I had at least three to five competing priorities. Looking back, I don't know how I managed. It seemed like the better I got, the more my workload increased. My hands were in everything. I had ideas to make improvements to streamline projects. At the onset, my ideas were not welcome, but they were considered as time went on. In meetings, my comments seemed to be under-appreciated, but I still kept sharing them. There were times that I provided solutions, and then someone else would repeat what I said, and they received credit for my ideas. I felt heavily scrutinized in the department. One day, our Chief Admissions Officer, pulled me to the side and said, "I appreciate your work and I am glad you're a part of the team... you should look into working for the EDI office!" Although, I believed she meant well, I was offended by the latter part of her statement.

Chapter 7:
Planted for Growth

I chose to bloom where I was planted.

She was the Chief Administrative Officer. She graduated from Vanderbilt and had family members who attended. Everyone knew and loved her. She was a great leader. Her specialty was identifying where employees should work based on their skillset. She gave her life to Vanderbilt. She worked long nights and weekends. She traveled to represent our department globally. She was the glue that held us together. She was diagnosed with cancer before I started. I couldn't see her in her glory, but the stories that were shared about her success are legendary. Sadly, she passed away approximately two years later. We were left with no real leadership. I already felt like everyone was my boss in our department and after she passed, my working environment worsened! People either chose to keep working, refused to work as hard, or sought promotion to her position. I knew they would never offer her former job to me. So, I continued to work relentlessly as I attempted to satisfy everyone's needs.

I used to vent to my suitemate about my competing projects, my experiences in meetings, and how I felt in the office. She felt the same way. She had a relationship with the Chief Administrative Officer. My suitemate took me under her wing and began to show me ways that I could do my work more efficiently. I valued our relationship. I trusted and admired her because she was a mother with three children and was respected in the office. The CAO spent a lot of time in our office talking with her about everything. It seemed that my suitemate always knew what was going to be announced before everyone else. She was good at making people feel comfortable around her. She shared some intimate details about her past work and life, and we became friends.

When Trump started his campaign for President, no one took him seriously. He spewed extremely derogatory comments about Mexicans, women, and minorities. There was no way that he would ever become the Republican nominee. In 2015, he was the topic of conversation everywhere... and my workplace was no exception. Our male department head even dressed up like Bill Clinton for Halloween to mock Hillary Clinton. The office found it funny; I found it unsettling. He knocked on office doors, with four fingers in the air, saying "Four more years," in a haunted tone. It seemed that Trump's campaign conjured the ugliness in several people.

I was on Twitter and found a photo of that department head standing in front of a life-sized dummy of Hillary Clinton being hung by a noose. The tweet was shared on the department head's personal Twitter and retweeted by an official Vanderbilt program within our department. His personal Twitter showed him grinning in the photo with a caption that linked him to our departmental hashtag. Clearly, they didn't think there was anything wrong with what he did, and they believed this behavior was representative of our department. Minimized incidents like this were indicative of the culture I experienced throughout my time in that department at Vanderbilt. People in power with no understanding of how their decisions affect the powerless.

I followed protocol and reported the tweets. The person I showed it too, shrugged their shoulders. Just one week later, that person talked about voting for Ben Carson. That was a lost cause. I knew that the photo didn't trigger them as it triggered me. So, I confided my thoughts to my suitemate. My suitemate printed the tweet and took it to the Marketing department. They quickly removed it. No one was reprimanded; it was as if nothing had happened at all. Later on, I questioned if I should have just left the tweet on the Twitter handle. I also wondered if the person I showed it too originally would've rather that I let it remain on social media.

Eventually, Trump was elected. I think that his presidency reminded everyone that racism and prejudice exist. I don't know how they didn't know this, but it seemed that the minorities of the office became closer during his term. My relationship with my boss, for instance, was always business; however, over time, even she opened up and became invested in who I was as a person.

Instances of racism at Vanderbilt and elsewhere appeared to be heightened. Unwillingly, I became the Al Sharpton of the office. Every time a Black person was killed by the police, and then I'd explain why their life mattered. When Colin Kaepernick kneeled, I had to be a sports expert. When Black people protested, my coworkers asked me why. It was exhausting. I was emotionally drained at work due to the climate of America and my home life. I had to do something for myself.

Therefore, I applied to two Doctor of Education (Ed.D.) programs, Lipscomb University and Tennessee State University. My suitemate spoke highly of Lipscomb; however, my first choice was Tennessee State University. I was so enamored with my husband's HBCU experience that I wanted one too. Lipscomb accepted me. Tennessee State called after I was already admitted to Lipscomb. I enjoyed the Ed.D. experience at Lipscomb but longed for the community that I experienced with my husband at his HBCU alma mater.

Finally, my husband was officially admitted to dental school. I was so proud of him. We were both enrolled in doctoral programs with a young child while managing our renters in Memphis. It was tough. At Vanderbilt, I finally got my stride; I had great performance reviews. My relationship with my boss evolved into a friendship. My suitemate moved into her own office and my peers sought my guidance and expertise to improve projects.

I was elected by my peers to serve on the Vanderbilt University Staff Advisory Council. This organization consisted of departmental representatives throughout Vanderbilt. We met monthly to discuss staff-related issues and worked to keep staff morale high. I thrived in this space. I was even elected to serve as the Communications Co-Chair. It seemed like the more resilient I became, the more I was tested. I felt like I had to prove my value, and I got tired of having to deal with it every day. So, I started applying for jobs and attending interviews. I used the connections I made with USAC to apply internally because I did not want to leave Vanderbilt. I was convinced that the issues I had were only in my department. I assumed that if I left my department, things would be better.

One day, a representative from a local HBCU contacted me on LinkedIn for a Director of Admissions position. We met for lunch, and the professional courtship began. A few months later, I had breakfast with his President and Provost. The Provost offered me an academic affairs position that was half of my current salary. I was insulted. It was a complete waste of my time.

Then I met with the President and a few other Senior leadership team members for the Director of Admissions role. I was excited; we hit it off immediately. They offered it, and then they decided not to hire for it. I was devastated. I interviewed with their team for six months for two positions that I never applied for.

Admittedly, the TSU EdD committee's lack of responsiveness and the interview time with the local HBCU left a bad impression.

I got pregnant with my second child while enrolled in the EdD program. We had a gender reveal party for him at my mentor's home, Rosetta Miller-Perry. I lovingly call her, Grandmier. Rosetta is the founder and CEO of the Tennessee Tribune Newspaper. She is also my brother-in-law's grandmother. He introduced me to her when we arrived in Nashville. My husband's older sister is an attorney, and her husband is a business owner. They met at Hampton University, an HBCU in Virginia. They have two girls. My husband is from Milwaukee. His mother is also a business owner, and his father is a salesman. He has two twin sisters that are younger than him. He is the middle child. My sisters and brothers do not have children. My husband and I are the first in our immediate family to have a little boy. He is a junior. Our son's gender reveal was at my Grandmier's home on my birthday. My graduation was on his first birthday. My son is a lovely child and his debut into the world was right on time.

I remember telling my boss that I was pregnant and that we had a gender reveal. Admittedly, I did not want a boy. I didn't think that I could handle the pressure of mothering a son. She told me that I would be a great mother and not to worry. However, Black males are disproportionately affected by daunting realities of living in the American society. According to the Pew Research

Center, Black men are six times more likely to be incarcerated than whites. Working in a highly political environment and constantly defending Black people being gunned down by police provoked me to action. I began to think of ways I could make things better. I accepted that I was having a son and recognized that Black girls deal with the same issues. In *Pushout,* Dr. Monique Morris discussed how Black girls are marginalized and punished at a higher rate than their white peers. What could I do to help my people feel accepted for who they are? I do not want my children to grow up in a world that claims to be threatened or afraid of their Blackness.

I completed my Doctor of Education degree while pregnant, working full-time, and with my husband enrolled in school. When I graduated, I felt so accomplished as I walked across the stage with my degree. I knew that I would be able to find a new job with my newly achieved credential. Nonetheless, it was harder than I felt it should've been. I began to think that the degree was doing more harm than good. After all, I now had more experience and education than most people in my office.

I began to network with anyone that would have lunch with me, Deans at Lipscomb, AVPs at Vanderbilt, business owners, and their friends. I literally had at least 10 lunch meetings a month between December 2018 and March 2019. Everyone wanted to help, but I was still stuck in a position where I felt disrespected, under-appreciated, and overlooked for advancement opportunities. I battled depression and my stamina was low after the baby. I assumed that my degree would help me feel accepted in my department, but my acceptance couldn't just be a feeling... it had to be a respected reality. I was treated like an asset everywhere except within the role that paid me. It was the weirdest feeling I ever experienced in my life. *They* wanted me to fail. I tried not to believe this notion and I continued to persevere.

While serving as the Communications Co-Chair for the Vanderbilt Staff Advisory Council, no one around me knew what I was going through. In fact, there were USAC members, particularly Black women, who wanted to work with me. They thought that I had it all together. They told me about the issues they endured in their departments. They assumed that since my title was, associate director, that I could make hiring decisions. Everyone had the same issues, but it seemed as though no one was able to help us. Admittedly, I never shared my issues with them. I felt like I had to be the positive one, although I was emotionally drained.

Eventually, I met mentors at Vanderbilt. One of them invited me to lunch events with other Black women at Vanderbilt. She was very down to earth and graduated from Tennessee State University with her Doctor of Education degree. Attending events with Black women at Vanderbilt made me feel good because I knew I wasn't alone. I benefitted from the community. However, I quickly realized that none of us had any "true" power. I had worked in leadership positions before. I had created positions and seen positions become created. I had reported directly to the CEO and sat in on Board meetings. However, I learned that it just doesn't work that way for us in traditional Higher Ed. It was clear that were all hired as tokens in our departments. Rosebeth Kanter (1997) formalized tokenism as a theory of organizational behavior. Kanter's theory asserted that individuals who represent less than 15% of the workplace are likely to experience psychological stress, even when they succeed in work performance. I was stressed and couldn't find true acceptance for myself, so I had to create my own community.

I started a blog, www.carjiescott.com. Initially, I focused on writing motivational posts and interviewing Black people who were doing great things in Nashville. I searched for Black-owned businesses and contacted the CEOs. It made me feel good to highlight them in the articles. In the midst of all the Black greatness I highlighted, I continued to hear the office banter about the lack of students from diverse backgrounds who were possibly interested in our department. Instead of allowing it to bother me, I created solutions. I volunteered to help recruit students from Meharry Medical College and participated in diversity orientation events. I wrote an eBook titled "How to Attend College for Free in TN." I figured this would be a great way to increase the pipeline of Black students attending college eventually. My lived experiences and data indicated that students from diverse backgrounds do not receive equitable access to quality education at the onset. This fact limited their opportunities to submit a competitive college application and creates a small pool of potential applicants.

I found myself spending time in spaces where I felt appreciated. I became a volunteer for The Equity Alliance. A non-profit organization led by Charlane Oliver and Tequila Johnson. They are a dynamic duo; I would call them the "Stacey Abrams" of Nashville. I was in awe as I watched them work and witnessed how in sync they were. I was asked to participate in the Tennessee State University Homecoming parade. I invited my sister-in-law to join me since she had graduated from TSU. We marched down Jefferson Street encouraging onlookers to vote. It was powerful. Charlane gave me access to the Equity Alliance email and mailbox. I met some great people in Nashville and throughout Tennessee. I became a member of the leadership team for the organization. I traveled to Memphis with The Equity Alliance and helped with their "Black Citizenship in Action" education program. This was the first time I was truly fueled by the service I provided instead of the money I earned.

I began to appreciate and value serving my community. Then I asked God, "How can I free myself from Vanderbilt?" It didn't seem as though He heard me. However, I kept reading my Bible, and I started listening to high-frequency law of attraction music. I did everything I could until I couldn't any longer. One afternoon, while working in my office, I felt a burning sensation in my side. The pain was indescribable. I went to the university clinic and was diagnosed with shingles. The doctor said that I was stressed. I was home for three days. I realized the effect of constantly fighting to be accepted had taken a toll my physical health. I vowed that I would no longer be pushed over or around at Vanderbilt [or anywhere else]. I no longer allowed my worth to be determined by people who didn't give a damn about me.

Finally, the CAO role was replaced by a new department head. The department head came in with an agenda and was determined to make changes. She was a graduate of our department. She developed a new relationship with my old suitemate. As an alumna, she continued relationships with existing employees. I carried on with my work. She hardly ever met with me. On one occasion, she called me by my boss's name. Perhaps she thought we looked the same since we were both Black women. It was unsettling and odd.

Persistently, I continued to thrive. My communications courses paid off. I was so glad that I utilized the constructive criticism from my boss to enhance my skill set. The Vanderbilt University Staff Advisory Council awarded me with the Communications Co-Chair of the Year award. They also awarded me with the Karen Dolan Spirit award, which is given to one USAC member who embodies the collegial spirit of the late Karen Dolan. I was also awarded as a Nashville Emerging Leader by the Nashville Chamber of Commerce for my work serving with TN Promise and my eBook, "Attend College for Free in TN." TN Promise is an organization that pairs mentors with students who are interested in attending local community colleges.

Back in my department, our new leader began to share her plans to improve the office with my former suitemate and other people in the office. It seemed as though she made time to talk with everyone often except my boss about her plans and me. She only talked with me one time about her ideas, and it was in a group setting. We were all originally told that everyone in the office would have to reapply for their jobs due to restructuring. My boss and I were left out. We were the only Black women in her office, and we were discriminated against. I had plenty of emails from our new leader that expressed gratitude for my work. Frequently, our new leader asked me to complete projects and for ideas regarding various processes. I didn't understand why I always heard about what she planned to do from someone else.

In all fairness, her placement into the CAO's former position was bothersome. I felt empathy for her. Everyone knew the CAO was sick. And, that department head who posed with the hanging Clinton figure, never created a contingency plan... go figure. So, the new person came in with a target on her back. Our department operated with too many bosses and not enough workers. The water cooler talk indicated that she had just been fired from her old job and had a chip on her shoulder. I didn't engage in it because I had my own fair share of career issues. Unbeknownst to her, I often took up for her, assuring people that she aimed to make things better. Speaking to us was the furthest thing from her mind as she was probably trying to exert her authority in the office.

Chapter 8:
Blooming Purposely

The result of blooming where I was planted

L et me be clear, yes there were pockets at Vanderbilt that reflected this culture. However, my situation does not reflect how all employees are treated throughout the University. I attended a Public Theology and Racial Justice Collaborative event hosted at the Vanderbilt Divinity School. I did not know what to expect. Admittedly, I assumed it would include academic talking heads, speaking a language that would require me to keep a dictionary app handy, and attendees who were racial justice experts claiming to advocate for inclusion but not actually doing the work.

Therefore, I attended because I wanted to silence my inner critic. The institute lasted one week. We checked in on Monday and started with Vanderbilt Collaborative Fellows giving us a Ted-style talk of the work they had done regarding Public Theology and Racial Justice. I was impressed.

Later, we attended an event hosted by Fearless Dialogues. At this event, we were all greeted with, "It is good to see you." Then, we practiced how to genuinely "see" the gifts in each other and the world around us. The experience was eye-opening, and it helped me let my guard down for the remainder of the week. It encouraged me to "see" and call out what I witnessed to cause real change in the world.

Every morning started with "morning centering." For me, morning centering was prayer, for others, it was meditation or reflection. A facilitator led each centering. During mealtime, I tried to sit at a new table to practice "seeing" new people.

We were able to choose tracks to further our understanding of Racist Governance or Radicalized Economics. I was interested in both tracks but ultimately chose Radicalized Economics because I am interested in learning more about Housing, Urban Development, and Gentrification. My tracks were led by Vanderbilt professors who were great at sharing their knowledge of the topics they presented while engaging us in group discussions.

After our tracks, we participated in processing salons, in which we continued our group discussion and built community. During these intimate thought-sharing groups, I came out of my shell and realized that the institute was not designed to teach me about Public Theology and Racial Justice. It was designed to encourage us to share our truths and engage in the work. The facilitators were effective at creating a safe space; and it turns out that the institute was the self-care I did not realize I needed.

Self-care is important if you work within education in any capacity and community is equally important. Before the institute, I answered the call to service and committed to volunteering for The Equity Alliance. However, I was afraid to share that I am a member of this community. Reflecting on my fear and realizing that my assumptions were not valid, I understood how I perpetuated the exact symptom I claimed immunity against.

In other words, because I continue to find and engage with a community of activists, I must share my activism too. I am grateful to have ended the institute with a new beginning, new challenges to pursue, new confidence, and a new covering.

Within my department, my teammates were antagonized. Everyone tried to please our new department leader so that they could keep their jobs. More work had been placed on all of us to meet her demands, and there was a ton of infighting and finger-pointing.

I decided to go to HR because hostility consumed our workspace. Deliberately, my boss was hardly involved with many processes. She was also left off emails and conversations relating to tasks that were assigned to our team. I presented a timeline of my time in the department to HR. I explained how we had no contingency plan after the CAO's death, although we knew it was coming.

The power dynamics were out of control because there was not an interim leader, and there were constant conflicts with the Directors. There were several meetings when the Directors had conflicting priorities for the team. I even showed HR the photo of the department head with the noose. I also expressed how our department needed true diversity and equity. The culture had been toxic my entire time in the department.

Let me be clear; I did not show the department head with the noose to "cancel" him. I showed it because I believed that our new HR representative was someone that I could trust to change the department's culture. The HR representative asked me what I thought should be done. I suggested that a diversity and inclusion officer be assigned to our department and the department head receive D&I training. I was not the only person who saw the tweet. I was simply the *only* person who was willing and courageous enough to say something about it.

September 11, 2019, the new department head called me into a meeting with another leader and I received Reduction in Workforce paperwork. This occurred two days after I spoke with HR. RIF paperwork is given to employees when their positions are eliminated. I believe this was retaliation. Vanderbilt intends that all employees who receive RIF paperwork can be reassigned to another position. The RIF packet includes positions that employees can apply for. In my instance, my position was split into five positions.

Therefore, it was hard for me to choose a position that fit my skill set. The director-level positions available included: a reporting role, an admissions role, and an operations role. I knew my boss, suitemate, and another employee were the dark horse candidates for those roles. The only other director-level position that I could've considered was a Diversity Recruiter position. However, I could not, in good conscience, apply for that role. The last three positions were not at the director level. All of the available positions contained my job responsibilities. So, I refused to apply for a position that was less than my skillset and would have resulted in a pay cut.

After all, I had accumulated four years at Vanderbilt and a Doctor of Education degree. My education exceeded all the applicants that were chosen for the roles. After reviewing the packet, the other leader told me that my position was to be eliminated, and I should speak directly to HR with questions. The other leader told me that I could choose to apply for another job in the department or elsewhere; and, if I do not get a job, I will be offered several weeks of severance and service pay. The conversation ended with a discussion regarding Vanderbilt's priority applicant status and the other leader told me to take the rest of the day off. The new department leader didn't utter a single word during the meeting. After the meeting, I said thank you and goodbye. I never returned to my full-time position at Vanderbilt.

Although my department leader told me that everyone would have to reapply for their jobs, only myself, my boss, and my suitemate were required to reapply. When I reviewed the jobs that were posted, I did not want to compete with my suitemate and my boss for positions in the department. I contacted HR and opted to leave altogether. Although I had priority applicant status, I did not apply for any jobs at Vanderbilt. My boss, suitemate, and co-worker got the positions that I assumed they would get. My co-worker did not have to apply for her position. However, my boss and suitemate had to apply and interview for their position. There are just some places that did not deserve me.

Just two years later, Black Lives Matter appeared on the department's website that I worked for. Although I know adding BLM to the website is performative, I believe that my time there helped to make a difference for future minorities. The department head who eliminated my role has reached out to me a few times since my departure. However, the department head who posed with the noose has not. I truly valued Vanderbilt and the relationships I built. It was one of the best experiences of my lifetime. I also *still* have a relationship with my boss and former suitemate. I wish them all the best.

Chapter 9:
Equalized Freedom

People will do whatever it takes to keep you when they value you.

N ews travels fast. Everyone began to reach out to me with job leads at Vanderbilt and elsewhere. However, I wanted to rest, I needed it. My husband was slated to graduate from dental school, my son was in daycare, and my daughter was in kindergarten. I finally had the house to myself, and I took advantage of it. I made friends from my service projects at The Equity Alliance and devoted more time to the organization. I wasn't ready to commit to a full-time position and decided to begin doing some consulting work. My first projects were at Vanderbilt, The Equity Alliance, and The Sunday School Publishing Board. I was proud of my ability to sell myself and book multiple contracts.

I continued interviewing Black people doing remarkable things in Nashville. My articles were published in the Tennessee Tribune Newspaper. I planned to do consulting work full-time. I did well and worked at my own pace. I felt as though I had stumbled upon something great. Then, I received a phone call from an AVP at Tennessee State University.

TSU had an opening for a Director of Admissions and Recruitment position. The AVP was pleasant. He made me feel welcome, and we had a great first interview. He invited me in for a second interview with his colleagues and members of his leadership team. One of the interviewers happened to be a classmate from my doctoral program. Everyone seemed pleased with me during the group interview. I was able to learn more about the role and shared what I could bring to TSU if they selected me for the role.

A week went by, and my husband mentioned that he had matched to the University of Florida for a Periodontist residency. After receiving the news from my husband, the AVP called and asked me to come in for an interview with the President. I was honest and shared the news about my husband with him, but he still advocated for me and arranged that I meet with the President for the final interview.

The President and I hit it off. She even mentioned that she had Googled my blog and was impressed by the work I was doing in the community. I was amazed that she had taken the time to get to know me beyond my resume. I shared all the success I had from previous roles and gave my vision for the Admissions and Recruitment department. If selected for the position, I knew I would get the job done and do it exceptionally well. However, my husband would be relocating in the fall. Since we had two young children, I would have to go with him. She still wanted me. I started in the role the following Monday. I was reminded that people will do whatever it takes when they value you. It meant a great deal to me that they still offered me the position. I recognized that they could have given it to anyone else, but they chose me, and I was determined not to let them down.

I was assigned a new team of 12 admissions and recruitment employees. It was an entirely newly hired team with only four existing members. I relied on the existing members for training, and I investigated how processes worked to make improvements. I documented everything and maintained a shared drive with all of our materials. I quickly realized that the operations needed to be streamlined to compete with other colleges. I spoke up about how our department compared with the other admissions teams I worked with.

I reflected on my experience when I applied to TSU for the Doctor of Education program. I was accustomed to the automated processes of the other schools I had worked for and I assumed that all admissions offices operated in a similar manner. I was disappointed to learn how disadvantaged my department was and quickly learned that other HBCUs had similar setbacks.

I witnessed my existing employees working from sunrise to sunset. For them, this was acceptable. However, I could not condone the lack of work life balance because I was unable to see the results that it brought our department. My assistant director of admissions arrived at work nearly two hours ahead of her shift. My East Tennessee recruiter left three hours after his assigned shift. My newly hired teammates were like sponges; they wanted to learn everything they could. Everyone, and I mean everyone on the team, was committed to the success of the department. However, we were all spinning in circles.

Our broken processes overshadowed our commitment. I was determined to fix our issues. My department was so antiquated in our processes that some of our original training included: creating an out of office message, how to save a file as a PDF, and how to use a shared drive. It was a great opportunity because I was able to share my knowledge and create trust with my direct reports. However, it was a steep learning curve, and it took time to change bad habits.

My AVP was pleased with our success. Just two weeks into the role, we processed 750 applications. This was a record for the department. My AVP quickly learned that I worked at a fast pace and was innovative. He appreciated my tenacity and trusted me to make things happen. My AVP hosted weekly huddles to share priority items. I hosted monthly meetings to inquire about ways to help my team get their work done. I was the Director; however, I also recruited and processed applications alongside my team. I wanted to understand how every process worked and how we could improve them. My teammates appreciated how invested I was and often came to me with their problems and suggested solutions.

In March, the Coronavirus hit, and we were all required to work remotely. Who would have imagined this would be our new normal? I guess my President and AVP knew something that I didn't even know. I created an on-campus schedule to manage the tasks that could not be handled in that manner. I requested laptops for my teammates. I launched a live front desk, as suggested by my assistant director, for incoming visitors. I facilitated weekly virtual recruitment events to target students interested in Tennessee State. I connected with social media influencers like Travis P. Jackson, CEO and Founder of HBCU Pride Nation and Robert Mason, CEO and Founder of the Common Black College Application to create and attend new events for their audiences. I created a communications strategy for inquiries, prospects, applications in progress, and submitted applications. I divided the work among each employee. Recruiters became national territory and project managers. Admissions associates were assigned students to service and received manual applications to process weekly. I created an environment for the team to work efficiently and their ideas are always valued. This is why we continue to be successful.

Although our new team had limited resources, and unpredictable obstacles we still managed to achieve great outcomes. We enrolled the highest number of first-time students in TSU's latest five-year history. Some say in TSU history, period. It was a significant rebound after my experience at Vanderbilt. I needed the win, and I was glad that I was able to accomplish it an HBCU.

However, our overall enrollment still needed to improve. Overall enrollment represents students registered for classes and returning to the college through graduation. My team oversaw newly admitted students. Whereas our campus partners: orientation committees, academic advising, residence life, and student services helped to retain students. I created great relationships with many of the department leaders. I have yet to meet any team or leader at TSU who does not want to assist students. However, I have met several colleagues who need more support to give the students the assistance they require.

Although my team was responsible for new admits, TSU was concerned about retaining students. We asked questions and volunteered to help with retention. We became club advisors, attended student led events, and connected students with campus partners. We went above and beyond to assist our students. Our work is never done. I still remind the team that our efforts are not in vain while encouraging them to prioritize their assigned tasks.

I learned that other departments had the same operational issues that my department had. I shared this with my teammates and department leaders. I tried to find solutions and support everyone. I witnessed the employees assigned at TSU doing their jobs well. The issue was the lack of automation and resources needed to do their jobs efficiently. The President was happy with my performance and I was asked to serve on numerous committees and continued to learn how to make improvements campus-wide.

Besides serving as TSU's Director of Admissions and Recruitment, I believe that I landed there to share how disadvantaged HBCUs are when compared to other institutions. It is unacceptable and needs to change. As a former trade school professional, I recognize the potential of HBCUs. If HBCUs implemented a business model and offered trade courses they could raise more money. After all, schools like ITT Tech, Anthem and Vatterott have closed down. There are thousands of students in need of training to get a career. Where are those students going to obtain an education? I would like to see HBCUs offer trade programs and begin to recruit trade school students. There are benefits to creating on-site beauty and barber colleges, auto and diesel mechanic shops, and daycares on campus. These programs can generate revenue for HBCUs and current students. Additionally, on-site businesses can provide student employment and help with retention efforts.

Money and resources are owed to TSU and other HBCUs. This money can be used to purchase customer relationship management systems (CRMs) that meet student service standards, attract and retain high caliber faculty and staff, produce quality marketing materials, improve and build more buildings, improve our athletic facilities, and provide scholarships to incoming and continuing students. Based on my experience, I strongly believe that the disparity is deliberate.

When the pandemic hit, Meharry Medical College was the first college to execute a COVID 19 response plan and began hosting testing centers throughout Nashville. However, Meharry was not the first to be given the vaccine. Dr. James Hildreth, the President and CEO of Meharry Medical College was appointed to the Vaccines and Related Biological Products Committee of the FDA. Dr. Hildreth voted for the Pfizer vaccine to be distributed for frontline healthcare centers. Fox 17 News Nashville (Dec. 2020) reported, "Meharry did not make the list for vaccines."

Tennessee State University is a public university and an HBCU. According to Fox 17 News Nashville (Dec. 2020), "State lawmakers found that since the 1950s, the University of Tennessee Knoxville has always received in full its annual federal land grant. That money was sent directly to the university but done differently for Tennessee State University. Unlike UT Knoxville, TSU's money was sent directly to the state treasury department, sparking an investigation lead by state lawmakers." There are many more accounts that indicate that HBCUs have not received the same number of resources and funding as PWIs.

Despite these deplorable facts and yes there are countless other stories like these, HBCUs have continued to thrive and produce some of the most influential Black leaders in history. And I must repeat this from my earlier chapter, HBCU alumni account for roughly 80% of black judges and 50% of black lawyers and doctors. Their students account for 25% of black undergraduates who earn degrees in science, technology, engineering, and mathematics. The fact is, if HBCUs didn't exist, we'd have to create them for Black people to obtain professional careers and community.

HBCUs are relevant and necessary. Kamala Harris was elected as the first female Vice President of the United States of America. She graduated from Howard University, an HBCU. Reverend Raphael Warnock was elected as Georgia's first Senator. He graduated from Morehouse College, another HBCU. Marilyn Mosby is the State's Attorney for Baltimore City. She is the youngest chief prosecutor of any American city and graduated from Tuskegee University, yes, it is another prestigious HBCU.

People will do whatever it takes when they value you. I currently serve as the Director of Admissions and Recruitment for

TSU while my husband is enrolled as a Periodontist Resident at the University of Florida. By the way, my husband is the first Black male Periodontist Resident at the University of Florida. We need lawmakers to recognize the value of HBCUs so that HBCUs are given the same opportunities as PWIs. More importantly, they need to acknowledge the excellence of minorities. We need to provide more opportunities for Black people to be successful in college and life. We must ensure that incoming students know about all of their college options so that they can attend the best college for them. We need to speak truth to power and work together to make our universities more inclusive and demand that HBCUs receive the money that is owed to them. We need more people to feel emboldened to do the right thing even when it seems impossible. Dear reader, we need you to accept yourself and own your story so that you can help make a difference in this world.

Bonus Chapter:
Where Do I *Want* to Go from Here?

As the Education Equalizer™, I will work with lawmakers to help more students who attended for-profit colleges get their loans forgiven. I will continue to advocate for minorities at PWIs and assist with their retention of minority students, faculty, and staff. I will help HBCUs receive the resources and funding required to provide students with a quality education. I will also partner with HBCU leaders and develop strategic plans so that their institutions will thrive. I will start a college scholarship and endowment fund. I will continue consulting and start a full-service firm for universities and related entities who need help with streamlining processes, general operations, and servicing students.

I will continue to equip students with the information they need to choose the best college for them. As minorities continue to become "firsts in their field," I will promote and host activities that honor their commitment and help them navigate uncharted territories. Lastly, I will continue writing books that provide invaluable information and my voice will remain immutable!

Epilogue

If you don't remember any other words in this book, remember this: "You are welcome, you are exceptional, and you are worthy. This is why, you are accepted!" If you do not believe it now, I hope this book has encouraged you to believe it because you already have everything you need to be accepted. Until you believe that it is already within you, you will continue searching for acceptance from people and places that do not deserve you anyway. I challenge you to state the following "I" affirmations as you continue on your journey of acceptance.

Dr. Carjie Scott's Affirmations of Acceptance:

1. I own my story.

2. I will follow a new path even if it's uncomfortable.

3. I realize community and career are equally important.

4. I understand that losing can be a blessing.

5. I set boundaries and demand the respect I give.

6. I am prepared and I will not devalue myself.

7. I will continue to lift as I climb.

8. I will not succumb to imposter's syndrome.

9. I will not embrace survivor's guilt.

10. I don't need acceptance or validation from anyone else because I accept myself.

About the Author

Dr. Carjamin (Carjie) Scott, The Education Equalizer,™ has nearly two decades of higher-education leadership experience. Dr. Scott serves as an Author, Higher Education Executive, and Consultant.

Dr. Scott has publications in The Tennessee Tribune, Medium, xoNecole, and her personal blog and website www.carjiescott.com. Scott received the Karen Dolan Spirit Award and Communications Committee of the Year Award by the Vanderbilt University Staff Advisory Council.

Dr. Scott was also named one of Nashville's Emerging Leader finalist by YP Nashville and the Nashville Chamber of Commerce. Additionally, she was a nominee for Women who Rock Nashville. She earned the Admissions Voice to Voice Award and Admissions Excellence award while at Vatterott Career College.

Dr. Scott is married to Dr. Kerwin Scott, DDS and is the mother of their two beautiful blessings, Channing Scott and Kerwin Scott Jr. She loves reading, relaxing on the beach, and spending time with her family.

Glossary

1. **Admissions** - the office which allows students access or the granting of admittance into a college or university.

2. **Black Lives Matter** – a movement designed to end police brutality and overpolicing against African American people.

3. **Caste System** - a socioeconomic class structure that is determined by birth. Loosely, it means (in some societies), if your parents are poor, you're going to be poor, too.

4. **Classism** - prejudice against or in favor of people belonging to a particular social class.

5. **Cognitive Dissonance** - the state of having inconsistent thoughts, beliefs, or attitudes, especially as relating to behavioral decisions and attitude change.

6. **Customer Relationship Management (CRM)** – the technology used to manage the relationships between schools and students.

7. **Equal Emloyment Opportunity Commission** – the commission responsible for enforcing federal laws that make it illegal to discriminate against a job applicant or an employee because of the person's race, color, religion, sex (including pregnancy, transgender status, and sexual orientation), national origin, age (40 or older), disability or genetic information.

8. **Equity, Diversity, & Inclusion** - **Equity** refers to the fair and respectful treatment of all people. Valuing **diversity** means that we recognize and respect everyone's unique